W9-DFC-939

Written by Rob Alcraft

TOP THAT!™

CONTENTS

Introduction	4
The Probable History of Beer	5
The Beer Business	12
Making your own Beer	14
Drinking in Belgium	20
L'Abbaye des Rocs	22
Achel Trappist Extra	24
Saint Feuillien Tripel	26
Drinking in the Czech Republic	28
Lobkov	30
Zatec	32
Drinking in Denmark	34
Royal Red Erik	36
Tuborg	38
Drinking in Great Britain and Ireland	40
Adnams Suffolk Strong Bitter	42
Samuel Smith's Old Brewery Pale Ale	44
Shepherd Neame's Spitfire Premium	46
Guinness Original	48
O'Hara's Celtic Stout	50
Drinking in Germany	52
Weihenstephaner Kristall Weissbier	54
Maisel's Weisse Original	56
Schneider Weisse Original	58
Drinking in Holland	60
Gulpener Korenwolf	62
La Trappe Quadrupel	64
Lindeboom Pilsener	66
Drinking in Poland	68
Brok Premium	70

Zywiec Full Light	72
Drinking in the United States of America	74
Alaskan Smoked Porter	76
Brooklyn Lager	78
Dixie Beer	80
Goose Island IPA	82
Samuel Adams Boston Lager	84
Drinking in Mexico	86
Dos Equis Amber	88
Corona Extra	90
Sol	92
Drinking in China	94
Sun Lik Beer	96
Tsingtao	98
Drinking in India	100
Bangla	102
Cobra	104
Lal Toofan	106
Drinking in Japan	108
Asahi Dry	110
Kirin	112
Drinking in South America	114
Quilmes	116
Brahma Chopp	118
Drinking in Africa	120
Castle Lager	122
Windhoek Lager	124
Casablanca	126
Conclusion	128

BEERS OF THE WORLD IS NOT
AUTHORIZED BY ANY OF THE
BREWERS MENTIONED.

Next time you sink your face into a glass of warm beer, or if you prefer it cold, swig it half frozen from an icy bottle, you're probably getting closer to the origins of civilization than you realize. For beer may have been partly responsible for the first urge of humans towards settlement, and civilization.

The theory isn't as unlikely as it might sound. Why did the first ancient hunting and gathering societies bother to settle down? Some historians and archaeologists now argue that they had discovered beer—and must have been in need of some vital ingredients to make more of it. One of those ingredients was barley, used to make malt. To grow barley you need fields—in short, you need agriculture—for successful agriculture you need to stay put, and become civilized.

It's a sobering thought, if you're in need of one, that we might owe civilization in all its glory, from the hamburger and the widget to Australian rules football, not to brains, nor even organized religion, but to beer.

It's fitting, then, that beer is still so popular that nearly every country in the world has its own version of the beautiful drink. Welcome to the world of beer.

THE PROBABLE HISTORY OF BEER

For as long as there has been civilization there has been beer—probably. Humans have known how to make it in various forms for at least 10,000 years.

The Sumerians, who ruled the ancient cities of Ur and Babylon in what is now Iraq, were some of the earliest brewers.

Writings from around 4000 BC record how beer was made from mashed bread, and that drinkers felt exhilarated and blissful. Perhaps unsurprisingly, this kind of beer had to be drunk through a straw to filter out the unpleasant mashed up sediment.

Beer was important enough to be mentioned in one of the earliest written set of laws to survive, decreed by the Babylonian king, Hammurabi. These laid down a beer ration based on social status. An ordinary worker got two quarts a day while a high priest received five quarts a day. The punishment for offering poor-quality beer was death by drowning.

BEER FOR THE DEAD, AND THE FIRST BAR

The ancient Egyptians, who used beer in medicine and as part of worship, were also skilled and enthusiastic brewers. Each class in

Egyptian society was allowed a different quality of beer, and it was so important it was often used as wages. Beer was also included in the tombs of the dead, to aid the journey into the afterlife.

The Romans, however, were less enthusiastic about beer—they only drank it when they couldn't get wine. Nonetheless, beer brewing thrived at the outer reaches of the empire—in northern Europe, France and Britain. The Romans also built the first rest houses for travelers, addresses marked by a vine above the door. In towns these rest stops were called tabernae, and they were effectively the world's first bars.

BEER AND THE CHURCH

By the Middle Ages beer, at least for those who could afford it, had become a vital part of the diet. The ales of the time were rich sources of nutrition, particularly at a time when drinking water was often downright dangerous.

Monks were very enthusiastic about brewing—perhaps because they were allowed to consume several quarts when fasting. They began a tradition of monastic brewing that continues to this day, brewing some of the best—and strongest—beers around. Monks would often brew not only for their own use, but for pilgrims and visitors, and some basically ran monastery bars. Brewing became a large and profitable business for the church.

LAGER, LAGER

It was monks who introduced one of the most important innovations in beer making—lagering. At this time this meant storing beer in cool caves and cellars, so that the beer would keep and its flavor would be improved.

HOPS AND HALLUCINOGENS

Modern drinkers tend to think that all beers will have some element of hoppy bitterness, but hops were probably first introduced to the process in around the tenth century. Before hops were used, brewers tried various vegetables, herbs, fruit, and other oddities to flavor beer. The Germans were particularly resistant to hops, using everything from juniper berries, oak bark, wormwood and aniseed, to rosemary, Saint John's wort, pine roots, and henbane.

Many ingredients were experimented with, lots of which turned out to be poisonous—it is now known that henbane releases hallucinogens during the brewing process. Unsurprisingly, a huge number of superstitions surrounded brewing— bad beer was even blamed on "brew witches," who were drowned or burned.

Fortunately for beer drinkers everywhere, the hop not only gave a good flavor and stopped the beer being sickly sweet, it also helped preserve it. Soon the use of hops became universal and for the first time beer became something that drinkers of today might recognize.

Perhaps mindful of their past mistakes with ingredients some German states introduced the Purity Law in 1516, which required that only malt, hops and water be used to make beer. This brewing tradition is still proudly upheld by most German brewers.

THE ODIOUS AND LOATHSOME SIN OF DRUNKENNESS

Beer was not popular with everyone. Throughout history, authorities of various descriptions have attempted to get people to drink less beer. Even the ancient Egyptians wrote that they had problems with widespread drunkenness. While in tenth-century Kent, in England, King Edgar restricted the number of ale houses to one per village. Even early monks were being warned against drunkenness—perhaps difficult since they were often provided with up to five quarts of beer a day.

The problem only worsed. In thirteenth-century Europe, the quality of water declined as the population grew and towns became bigger. Anyone who could afford it drank beer instead. The problem continued for centuries—the English Parliament of 1606 felt moved to pass an act to suppress "the odious and loathsome sin of drunkenness". It didn't work.

SALOONS AND PROHIBITION

In the US, beer—and whiskey—proved just as popular. During the frontier days so many saloons opened up there was around one to every 200 people. To compete for a limited pot of profit many saloon owners introduced gambling and prostitution to supplement their beer revenue.

The saloon, and drink, were regarded by many as evil. There was even an Anti-Saloon League, and the stage was set for Prohibition. But Prohibition, like all the anti-beer laws through history, did not work. It is estimated that annual beer consumption fell by only a third during Prohibition, and that, at the time of his arrest, the notorious gangster and bootlegger Al Capone was earning $60 million a year from activities which included the sale of illegal alcohol. The world, it seems, was stuck with beer.

THE BEER BUSINESS

Until the nineteenth century brewing was predominantly a local and small-scale business. Then came steam power. For the first time beer could be made and moved in large quantities. Cheap, mass-produced bottles—with caps —were introduced in the 1890s. Also, there was another vital development for beer— refrigeration. For the first time, lager beers, which need fermentation temperatures between 39-50°F (4°C and 10°C) and which could often only be brewed in winter or in deep ice cellars, could be brewed at any time of year.

REVOLUTIONARY LAGER

Another nineteenth-century brewing revolution came from the European town of Pilsen, in the Czech Republic, where the first pilsner beers were brewed in the 1840s. These beers were clear and golden, and showed off well in the new glasses and bottles. Today this beer style—or versions of it—is the most commonly drunk beer in the world.

DEAD OR ALIVE?

The best beer is a live product— a little yeast or sugar is added before bottling or kegging, which continues to ferment, or condition, the beer until it is drunk. This process can, depending on the brew, add fizz, strengthen alcohol, and smooth the flavor of the beer.

Large-scale brewers found conditioned beer was more difficult and more expensive to make. Often, mass-market beers skip the conditioning step altogether, and the beer is pasteurized to kill any yeasts left alive and to stabilize the product. To add fizz, the beer is carbonated by pumping in gas.

During the twentieth century many styles and flavors of beer began to disappear as mass-market techniques were applied to brewing. Smaller breweries in Europe and America closed or were bought out, and many unique beer styles were lost.

In Britain, only a seemingly eccentric group called CAMRA (the Campaign for Real Ale) tried to fight the trend threatening to kill old-style English beer. In the US however, craft and real ale and lager is at last enjoying a renaissance.

MAKING YOUR OWN BEER

The ancient skill of brewing is not as mysterious as it might seem. It's relatively easy and cheap to make tasty beer in only a few hours. Start with English-style ale as it is more straightforward to make than lager.

THE KIT

You'll need to boil, mix, ferment and bottle to make beer. Start by getting hold of a re-useable kit—they don't cost much. You'll also need to start collecting beer bottles. The 6 gallon (22 l) brew explained here will need 48, 12 fl oz (340 ml) bottles.

A typical kit contains:
8 gallon (30 l) fermenting bucket
8 gallon (30 l) bottling bucket
Bottling tap
Bottle capper
Hydrometer (you don't need this if using extracts)
Thermometer
Fermentation lock
Siphon equipment
Bottle brush
Cleaning solution

BE CLEAN

In the Middle Ages people used to put bad beer down to brew witches spoiling the batch—now we know that problems are caused by wild yeast in the air and bacteria messing up the fermentation process. Clean and sterilize everything before you use it. Don't use any scented cleaning agents.

INGREDIENTS

Malt extract
Use malt extract, as this will make your first brew easier. You need around 1 lb (450 g) of malt extract per 1.2 gallon (4.5 liters) of water, although adding more will give a richer, fuller-bodied beer. Avoid extracts with corn or maize in them.

Water
Don't underestimate the importance of water to your brew— one of the secrets of some of the best brewers in the world is the water they use. If water from your faucet tastes good to you, it will make good beer; if it doesn't, use bottled water.

Hops
The first time you make beer you may prefer to use a malt extract with added hops. You will get a better beer if you use an unhopped malt extract, but the brewing process is rather more complicated.

Hops, bought whole or as pellets, can be added at three stages during brewing, depending on your taste. Different varieties of hop have different levels of bitterness.

How many you add depends on their level of bitterness, and how bitter you like your beer. Follow the guidelines provided with the hops you buy—they will have a bitterness value, often expressed as a percentage.

Yeast

First time round use a dry ale yeast. Ale yeasts work above 53°F (12°C). You will be making top-fermenting beer, where the yeast prefers to live at the top of the fermenting tank.

BREWING

The Wort

The wort is the boiled malt, hops and water.

1. Boil 2 gallons (9 l) of water. Add to the fermenting bucket, and let it cool.

2. Next boil another 4 gallons (14 l) of water. When it boils, add the malt extract, stirring well. Make sure it is all mixed in and doesn't stick. Stir regularly. At this stage the first of two or three lots of hops would normally be added, but it is easier to use a hopped malt extract for a first brew.

The Yeast

3. While the brewing water boils rehydrate the yeast; add it to a cup of warm pre-boiled water (95-104°F /35-40°C) in a jar, cover and let it stand for fifteen minutes.

4. Next add a spoonful of malt extract or sugar to a cup of water and boil it. When this has cooled to 95-104°F (35-40°C), add it to the yeast jar. Check it after thirty minutes—it should be foaming. If it isn't, it's dead and you will need to prepare another batch of yeast.

5. Boil and stir the wort for around fifteen minutes, watching to make sure it doesn't boil over. With hopped malt extract this short boil time is all that is needed.

6. When the wort stops foaming you have reached the hot break stage— make sure you wait for this point. Take the wort off the boil, and cool it as quickly as possible by placing the boiling pot into cold water— but keep the pot covered to prevent contamination. Take this step seriously—cooling the wort quickly without contamination is very important for the flavor of the beer.

7. Add the yeast to the water in the fermenting bucket.

8. Pour the cooled wort into the water in the fermenting bucket. You should aim to have the mixed wort and water at a temperature of around 64-72°F (18-22°C). Splash the wort into the fermenting bucket as this will help to add oxygen for the yeast.

Fermentation

9. With the wort, water and yeast in the fermenting bucket, put the lid on and place the bucket somewhere out of the way and out of the sun, ideally at a temperature of around 64–72°F (18–22°C).

When you have moved the fermenting bucket put the airlock in, then leave it.

10. This is the time to clean all brewing equipment, ready for sterilizing when you next brew.

11. Fermentation will begin within a few hours, and the airlock will bubble steadily. Leave the beer alone for at least two weeks by which time the first fermentation will have stopped.

Bottling

12. The beer needs to be primed before bottling. This means adding sugar to begin a secondary

fermentation which will take place in the bottles. The live beer will condition itself inside the bottles and become carbonated, ready for you to drink. For 6 gallons (22 l) of beer you will need around 4 oz (110 g) of sugar dissolved in a cup of boiled, warm water. Use a sterile bottling bucket. Add the priming sugar, then siphon in the beer from the brewing bucket. Don't start the siphon with your mouth as this will contaminate the beer with bacteria and give you sour beer. Start the siphon with sterile water.

13. Cap the filled bottles and store at 64–75°F (18-24°C). A layer of yeasty sediment will form at the bottom of each bottle. The beer will be ready to drink in around two weeks.

HOW DID YOU DO THAT?

Every time you brew, keep notes on quantities, ingredients, and times. If it's a good brew you can repeat it; if it isn't you can ensure you don't repeat the same mistakes.

DRINKING IN BELGIUM

The Belgians brew some of the best and most distinctive beers in the world—and treat beer with the respect that some countries reserve only for wine. Beers are often served in a distinctively shaped glass. It could be anything from a champagne-style flute for Frambozen, to a squat tumbler for Hoegaarden.

This small country still has over 100 breweries. The country's Trappist breweries—where monks still sometimes serve as head brewer—are some of the most respected. They produce ales and lagers to age-old recipes.

Lambic beers are most popular around Brussels. Lambic beer uses an ancient brewing method—once universal among brewers—which relies on wild yeast in the air for spontaneous fermentation. Lambic beers are cloudy, have a good sour flavor and may be aged for up to a year. One style of lambic sold in many Brussels bars is gueuze, which is a blend of old and new lambic beers.

Each region of Belgium still has a traditional brewing style, ranging from the red beers of west Flanders to the seasonal Saison beer favored in Wallonia.

L'ABBAYE DES ROCS

The Abbaye des Rocs brewery started as a co-operative in 1979, producing just 13 gallons (50 l) of beer every two weeks. It now brews five different beers, with half the product going for export. This strong, deep amber L'Abbaye des Rocs is brewed using seven types of malt and three kinds of hop. It has a strong reputation for maturity and flavor.

STRENGTH	9% abv
BEER STYLE	Belgian ale
ORIGIN	Montignies-sur-Roc, Belgium
TASTE	rich and malty, with a balanced sweetness

Trappist beer, which is typically malty and strong, is only brewed by Cistercian monks, or it doesn't qualify as Trappist. This monastic brewing tradition goes back to the Middle Ages—Achel's monastery had a brewery until it was commandeered by the Germans during World War One. The present brewery, set up with money from the sale of abbey lands, has been brewing since 1991. It is one of only six Trappist breweries now operating in Belgium and brews strong, complex beers in the quality Trappist tradition.

STRENGTH 8% abv
BEER STYLE Trappist ale
ORIGIN Achel, Belgium
TASTE dry, full and strong, with malt and hops

Saint Feuillien Tripel is named after an unfortunate Irish monk who was decapitated in AD 655. Made in a family-owned brewery, this strong, amber-colored beer is top fermented in the same way as English ale. The beer is then cooled—lagered—for six weeks before being aged for a further three weeks when it is then bottled. This involved brewing process, which uses spring water from beneath the brewery buildings, gives Saint Feuillien Tripel its rich, complex flavor.

STRENGTH	8.5% abv
BEER STYLE	Abbey tripel
ORIGIN	Le Roeulx, Belgium
TASTE	rich, fruity malt, and hops

DRINKING IN THE CZECH REPUBLIC

Today, most lager in the world pays homage to the Czech brewing tradition—even to the point of borrowing famous Czech beer names such as Budweiser—a beer originally from the Czech town of Budweise.

Brewing in the Czech Republic is an ancient tradition, but it has been put under pressure from foreign buyouts since the fall of communism in 1989. Many brewery buildings date back to the nineteenth century, and some breweries still make their own malt. Two of the most famous and widely available brands of Czech beer are Pilsner Urquell and Budweiser Budvar—which are both fine and well-respected beers in their own country.

In the Czech Republic beer is often sold on draught—pivo—and drunk with food or a meal. The country's bars are mainly a place for men and some very heavy drinking.

The Lobkowicz brewery in the west of the country has a brewing tradition which goes back to 1466. The brewery was nationalized under the Communist government, and it was only returned to its owners—the Lobkowicz family—in 1992.

Lobkowicz uses traditional pilsner brewing techniques, such as open fermentation tanks, and world-renowned saaz hops. This Lobkov beer is the brewery's export brand.

STRENGTH	4.8% abv
BEER STYLE	pilsner
ORIGIN	Vysocky Chlumec, Czech Republic
TASTE	sweetish malt and hop

ZATEC

The town of Zatec, in the northwest of the Czech Republic, is an ancient feature of Bohemian beer tradition. The clay, iron-rich soils of this area are renowned for its saaz hops, which are not particularly bitter but very aromatic. Reputed to be the best hops in the world, saaz hops are a vital ingredient in the dry, aromatic lagers popular in this part of the country.

STRENGTH	4.6% abv
BEER STYLE	pilsner
ORIGIN	Zatec, Czech Republic
TASTE	hoppy, clean flavor

For the ancient Danes, paradise was a great hall where the dead passed their time drinking ale—supposedly squeezed from the udders of a she-goat and served in the skulls of their enemies.

The Danish are still keen on beer, and drink more of it per head than most other countries in Europe. The country is also home to the Carlsberg/Tuborg empire—one of the biggest brewers in the world. The company's export beers are not particularly exciting today, but, in the past, one innovative Carlsberg brewer was responsible for discovering—and isolating—brewing yeast varieties when everyone else was still brewing in the old hit-and-miss fashion. The brewer transported the first batch of pure brewing yeast personally, by stagecoach, from over 600 miles away in Bavaria. Most of the time he carried the yeast under his top hat.

Most beer in Denmark follows the pilsner style, but there are still many old and unusual styles of beer. One traditional ale is a dark, almost opaque, beer called Hvidtol. It is very lightly fermented and often has sugar added to give it a texture and flavor reminiscent

of drinking chocolate. Hvidtol has several versions depending on the season, but the Jule, or Christmas, version is one of the sweetest.

It's traditionally drunk with savory rice pudding as a starter for Christmas dinner and a glass is often left out for Santa's elves.

This beer is named after Erik the Red, the Viking who discovered Greenland in AD 982. Legend has it that, on landing, Erik and his crew brewed beer to celebrate. What color that beer was isn't known, but this beer, as its name suggests, is red—it is colored with fruit and berry juices. Red Erik is brewed by Ceres—a company started in the 1850s which is now part of a larger brewery group.

STRENGTH	6.5% abv
BEER STYLE	lager
ORIGIN	Aarhus, Denmark
TASTE	slight malt flavor

Tuborg, with its partner company Carlsberg, produces more than three quarters of the beer drunk in Denmark. Since its inception in 1873, Tuborg has been an export-orientated company, and that partly explains why its first location was on the Copenhagen waterfront. Its international-style beers, like this Tuborg green, tend to be light with modest flavor.

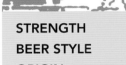

STRENGTH	5% abv
BEER STYLE	lager
ORIGIN	Copenhagen, Denmark
TASTE	light and mildly hoppy

DRINKING IN GREAT BRITAIN AND IRELAND

According to ancient Welsh chronicles, the English used to go into battle drunk. In fact, some historians suggest that the Normans won the Battle of Hastings in 1066 because the English, having beaten the Vikings a few days before, were either drunk or incredibly hung over from the celebrations.

English beer is traditionally a style of beer known to the rest of the world as ale. It is a top-fermenting beer because the yeast floats and foams as it ferments. The best ale owes much to the early monastery brewers of the Middle Ages who enthusiastically perfected the art of brewing, drinking beer for its food value as much as anything else. These brewers never turned to lager because Britain's climate never really got cold enough.

Ireland, Scotland, and Wales also have a tradition of ale brewing, reinforced first by monastery brewers and then by English influence. Ireland is known now for Guinness, but also has its own style of red ales. Scottish ales tend to be darker with more malt than English beer.

ADNAMS SUFFOLK STRONG BITTER

The Adnams Sole Bay Brewery in the Suffolk seaside town of Southwold has been owned and run by the Adnams family since 1872. Of the two brothers who originally bought the brewery, one was later eaten by a crocodile in Africa.

Adnams brews distinctive full-flavor beers using old English hop varieties such as fuggles, and its bottled output includes a strong ale called Broadside.

STRENGTH	4.5% abv
BEER STYLE	bitter
ORIGIN	Southwold, UK
TASTE	distinctively dry, hoppy, and bitter

SAMUEL SMITH'S OLD BREWERY PALE ALE

Samuel Smith's, founded in 1758, is one of the few independent breweries left in England. It still uses square stone tanks in the fermentation process—a regional style of brewing that gives Samuel Smith's beer its distinctive smoothness and creamy, long-lasting head. The brewery is proud of its reputation for tradition and quality—even its strain of yeast dates from the 1900s.

STRENGTH	5% abv
BEER STYLE	pale ale
ORIGIN	Tadcaster, UK
TASTE	rich, creamy malt, and hops

Shepherd Neame, which claims to be the oldest brewery in England, was founded in 1698 by a captain in the Cinque Ports Militia. A more recent brew, Spitfire Premium, was first produced in 1990 to commemorate the fiftieth anniversary of the Battle of Britain. The beer is gold in color and hoppy in taste.

STRENGTH	4.5% abv
BEER STYLE	mild ale
ORIGIN	Faversham, UK
TASTE	lingering, well-balanced malt, and hops

GUINNESS ORIGINAL

The Guinness story really begins in 1759 when Arthur Guinness signed a 9,000-year lease on an abandoned brewery in Dublin. Today Guinness is brewed in 51 countries and sold in 150. One of the best-known beers in the world, 1,883,200,000 glasses of the black stuff are sold every year. Guinness's dark color and roasty bite come from the roasted barley malt which is one of its main ingredients. This bottled Guinness original is probably the beer closest in flavor to the original eighteenth-century concoction.

STRENGTH	4.3% abv
BEER STYLE	stout
ORIGIN	Dublin, Ireland
TASTE	smooth, toasted and bitter

O'HARA'S CELTIC STOUT

The Carlow Brewery only started in 1998, but O'Hara's Celtic Stout has already gained a reputation for quality and taste—it won a brewing industry gold medal in 2000. The O'Hara brothers who run the brewery aim to revive the ancient brewing tradition of Ireland—which stretches back at least to the first century AD when the Greek, Dioscorides, tells of Irish chiefs drinking a malt liquor called curmi.

STRENGTH	4.3% abv
BEER STYLE	stout
ORIGIN	Carlow, Ireland
TASTE	roasty malted, nutty, and hoppy

DRINKING IN GERMANY

Germans have been brewing beer for more than 1,000 years. The ancient German Teutons used beer as a sacrifice to the gods. Today, no one drinks more beer than the Germans who consume more than 34 gallons (131 l) per head a year.

The center of Germany's brewing tradition is the northern state of Bavaria, which still contains more than half of the country's 1,200 breweries. Bavaria is also the origin of the Reinheitsgebot—the beer purity law. Imposed in 1516, it states that beer must contain only malt, hops and water. Many

German brewers still proudly abide by the purity laws, rejecting added brewing sugars and preservatives widely used in other countries.

Most beer is still brewed for the local market, and Germany doesn't have a "national" beer. Drinkers often stick loyally to traditional regional styles brewed nearby, and drinking habits also change with the season. Bock-style beers are still often thought of as springtime beers, and are traditional around Einbeck and Munich. Dunkel and dobblebock are also Munich styles,

but they are linked with winter. Dusseldorf is known for Altbier, a beer similar to English ale.

House breweries—where beer is brewed on the premises—have been a feature of German life since the Middle Ages. Beer gardens are also popular. The extent of the

Germans' love of beer is only really obvious at the world-famous Oktoberfest, a 70,000-seat tented beer festival held in Munich. Originally a wedding party and horse race that got out of hand, the Oktoberfest is now one of the world's premier beer celebrations.

WEIHENSTEPHANER KRISTALL WEISSBIER

Weihenstephaner can lay claim to being the world's oldest brewery, having been in operation since 1040. Kristall Weissbier is Weihenstephaner's leading beer, and its fermentation process is a closely guarded secret. Brewed with a mix of hops, wheat, and barley malt, it has a crystal-clear gold appearance.

STRENGTH	5.4% abv
BEER STYLE	wheat beer
ORIGIN	Freising, Germany
TASTE	Light, wheat flavor with a hint of spices

PREMIUM BAVARICUM

BAYERN

Weihenstephaner

KRISTALL
WEISSBIER

BRAUEREIABFÜLLUNG

THE WORLD'S OLDEST BREWERY

Maisel have been brewing since 1894. This is a bottle-conditioned beer. Unfiltered and cloudy, it is brewed using wheat as well as barley malt, and what brewers call top-fermenting yeast. They are the same kinds of yeast used for English ales, and this beer has the fruity depth of flavor found in ale.

STRENGTH	5.4% abv
BEER STYLE	wheat beer
ORIGIN	Bayreuth, Germany
TASTE	fruity with some good wheat and yeast flavors

SCHNEIDER WEISSE ORIGINAL

Schneider Weisse Original comes from Bavaria's oldest Weizen brewery and is among the classical German hefeweizens. As with many hefeweizens, it can have a banana and vanilla aftertaste. This beer is unpasteurized and unfiltered, and the top-fermenting yeast resettles on the bottom. It has a light but firm body and can prove refreshing.

STRENGTH	5.4% abv
BEER STYLE	wheat beer
ORIGIN	Kelheim, Bavaria, Germany
TASTE	sweetish malt and hop

DRINKING IN HOLLAND

Not everyone realizes that both gin and Heineken originate in the Netherlands. Gin was first distilled in the 1600s, making it about the same age as Grolsch. Heineken is more recent, but has still become part of life across the world. First brewed in Amsterdam in 1865, the Heineken brewery is now one of the largest beer companies in the world.

Dutch export beers tend to be pale lagers, but at home even the big brewers offer well-flavored, abbey-style beers, bocks, and dark lagers. The high-quality, speciality beers are influenced by the brewing traditions of Germany and Belgium.

The Netherlands has a strong café and bar culture—Amsterdam particularly is known for its brown cafés, so called because of their tobacco-stained paint, many of which are hundreds of years old. They fullfil the same vital role in Holland as the pub does in England. One favorite order is a "kopstoot" or headbutt, a beer with a gin chaser.

"Taking a Dutchman's draught" refers to the sizeable glasses Dutchmen once favored for their beer.

GULPENER KORENWOLF

The word Korenwolf roughly translates as corn wolf, or hamster, and is appropriate to this beer which is brewed with wheat, rye, barley, and oats. Coriander is also sometimes included. It is blond and cloudy with suspended yeast. The Gulpener brewery is also known for a bitter pilsner lager called X-pert.

STRENGTH	5% abv
BEER STYLE	wheat beer
ORIGIN	Gulpen, Holland
TASTE	light, refreshing beer with some sourness and spice

LA TRAPPE QUADRUPEL

La Trappe Quadrupel is a strong, rich ale brewed at Schaapskooi, a Trappist monastery in the southern Netherlands. Trappist beers are, typically, malty, rich and dark. La Trappe Quadrupel is the strongest beer on offer from Schaapskooi. Dobbel and tripel (designations based loosely on their comparative strengths) are also available.

STRENGTH	10% abv
BEER STYLE	Trappist ale
ORIGIN	Schaapskooi, near Tilburg, Holland
TASTE	rich and malty

LINDEBOOM PILSENER

The Lindeboom (Linden tree) is a respected family-run brewery founded in 1870. It produces a range of lagers, including an amber-red Vienna-style lager called Gouverneur. The brewery is best known for the Lindeboom Pilsener, a dry and lightly hoppy, bock beer.

STRENGTH	5% abv
BEER STYLE	bock
ORIGIN	Neer, Holland
TASTE	dry and delicately hoppy

DRINKING IN POLAND

There's a story that when the Polish Pope Clement lay dying, he made an urgent utterance that sounded, at first, like the creation of a new saint. In fact, as those around him strained to hear the venerable man's last words they realized he was, in fact, asking for a beer.

The story is apocryphal but hints at the fact that drinking is a national pastime in Poland. It is telling that there is still no legal minimum drinking age, and many Poles have a prodigious appetite for alcohol of all kinds. They are known particularly for their vodka and there is a huge variety of clear and herb-flavored vodkas available.

Poles also have a long-standing relationship with beer. There are around seventy breweries, though many have recently been swallowed up by international brewers such as Heineken, South African Breweries, and Carlsberg.

The Polish preference is for light, hoppy lagers—and in a taste imported from Britain during the eighteenth century—also for strong, sweet and black Baltic-style porters. The tradition of local

beer is getting rarer, and some homegrown styles, such as a smoked wheat beer called Grodziskie, have disappeared.

Soviet-era drinking in Poland could be a depressing affair. In the big cities the only bars were very seedy and the drink of preference was hard spirit rather than beer. Hotel bars were for tourists and everyone else drank at home or in restaurants. Today, drinking in Poland is more convivial, and there are even a few brewery pubs producing their own beer.

Polish beer reflects neighboring Czech and German styles. This Brok beer is a hoppy, pilsner lager, a style of beer first brewed in Bavaria in 1842, and one that now dominates the world's beer market.

STRENGTH	5.2% abv
BEER STYLE	pilsner lager
ORIGIN	Koszalin, Poland
TASTE	crisp and hoppy

Zywiec is a small town in southern Poland, with a brewing history that stretches back to the Middle Ages. At one time only town dwellers were allowed to brew beer for profit, with peasants only permitted to brew beer twice a year, and then only for their own consumption.

The Zywiec brewery, which is now owned by Heineken, is at the foot of the Grojec mountains, and clear mountain water is an important ingredient in this distinctive malt and hop lager. The beer is sometimes known as the dancing couple because of the design on its label.

STRENGTH	5.7% abv
BEER STYLE	pilsner lager
ORIGIN	Zywiec, southern Poland
TASTE	dry and bitterish with a hoppy scent

The first American beers were maize brews made by Native Americans in what are now the southern states of the US. European-style beers arrived with the first settlers, who were used to drinking beer rather than water. In fact, beer was so important a contemporary report from *The Mayflower* explains that the Pilgrim Fathers were forced to stop at Plymouth Rock rather than carry on south because 'our victuals being much spent, especially our Beere'.

The first settlers planted hops and barley for malt, but also used corn, pumpkins, parsnips, oats, and even added walnut chips for flavor.

There was an ambiguous attitude to alcohol even in the 1600s, and in the New England colonies there were early attempts to provide, for the purposes of punishment, an exact definition of drunkenness. There were also early attempts at prohibition. One 1645 law which forbade the payment of wages in alcohol caused a strike. Nearly 300 years later there was real prohibition of course. The brewing and selling of alcohol went underground, spawning organized crime networks that exist to this day.

In the early 1980s the US, the largest consumer of beer in the world, had only around forty brewing companies in the entire country. Much of America's beer still reflects this big-business attitude, and is brewed in bland, pale lager style, and most big brands even have a light, diet version. Since the 1980s things have improved as craft brewers have gained in importance, and America is again learning to brew some of the world's best beer.

When the Alaskan Brewing Company started up in 1986 it was the only one in Alaska, and the first in Juneau since Prohibition. Its smoked porter is based on a Gold Rush-era style of beer still brewed in Germany. The malt was first smoked in a salmon smokehouse using local alder wood and glacier water. The smoke acts as a preservative. Alaskan smoked porter is a dark beer similar to German rauchbier. Brewed just once a year in the fall, like wine, the beer's taste develops and improves in the bottle.

STRENGTH	6.5% abv
BEER STYLE	porter
ORIGIN	Juneau, Alaska, USA
TASTE	a distinctively robust and smoky flavor

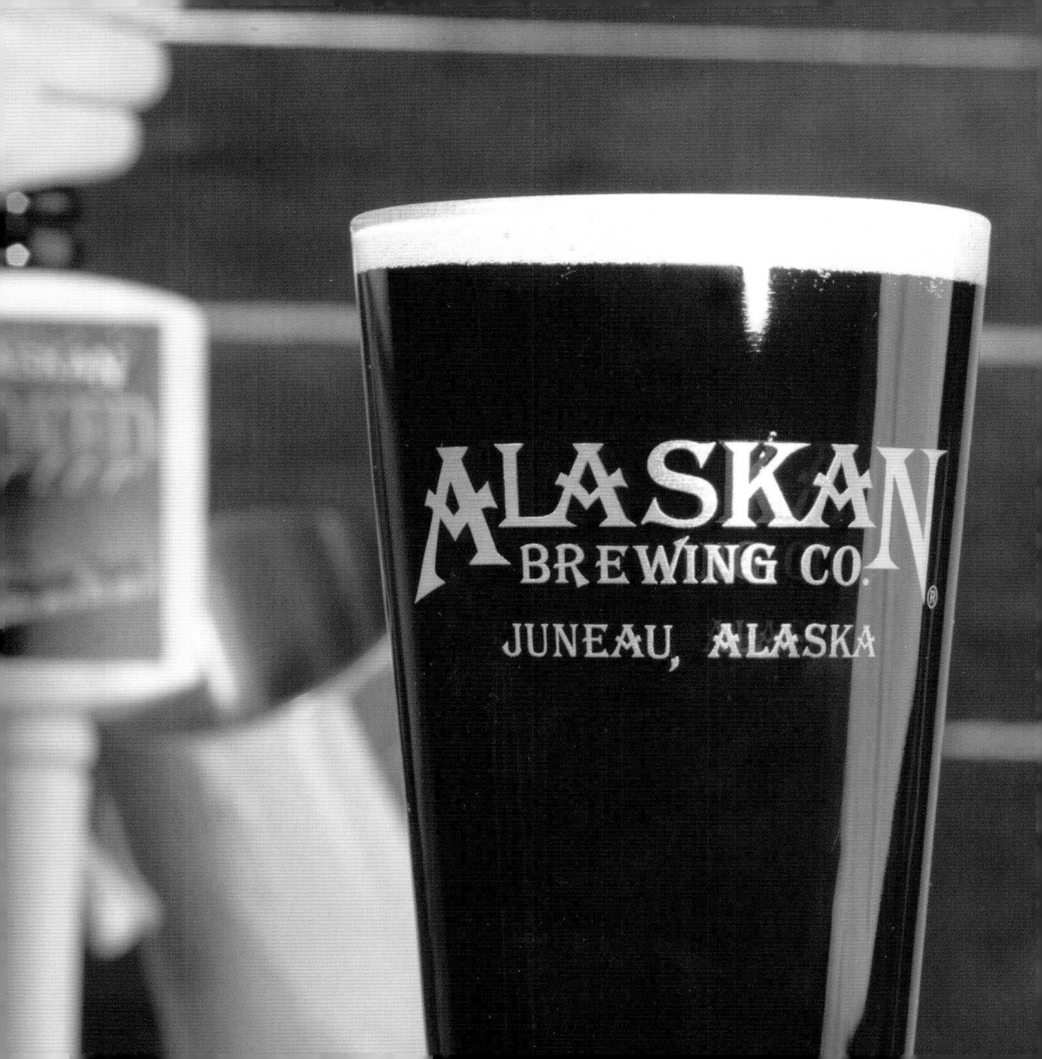
ALASKAN
BREWING CO.
JUNEAU, ALASKA

BROOKLYN LAGER

The Brooklyn brewery was founded in 1988 after
Steve Hindy started home brewing beer while
working abroad—often in Islamic countries where
he couldn't buy alcohol. Brooklyn lager, the
brewery's flagship label, is brewed to a recipe from
the days when Brooklyn, with its growing German
population, was the brewing capital of the East
Coast. The first batch of the lager was sold store-
to-store, by Steve Hindy himself. It is a distinctive
caramel-brown lager, with a bitter, hoppy taste
reminiscent of English-style ales.

STRENGTH	5% abv
BEER STYLE	lager
ORIGIN	New York, USA
TASTE	dry and hoppy

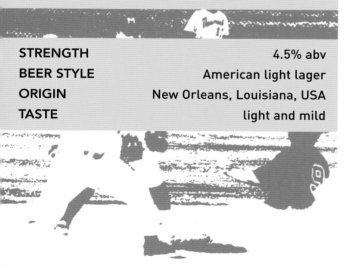

DIXIE BEER

The Dixie Brewing Company is that rare American thing, a brewery that has survived Prohibition, two world wars, and corporate takeover. Founded in 1907, the company produces a range of wood-aged beers, including Blackened Voodoo, and this American-style lager, Dixie Beer.

STRENGTH	4.5% abv
BEER STYLE	American light lager
ORIGIN	New Orleans, Louisiana, USA
TASTE	light and mild

Goose Island started as a brewpub, named after an island in the Chicago river. This dark golden, bottled beer is one result of its successful transition from pub to large-scale brewer. IPA stands for India Pale Ale, a beer style that dates from the days when beer exports to British India had extra hops added as a preservative.

STRENGTH	5.9% abv
BEER STYLE	India pale ale
ORIGIN	Chicago, Illinois, USA
TASTE	dry, with hoppy, bitter taste

The Boston Beer Company was founded by a sixth-generation brewer in 1985. Samuel Adams lager is brewed from an old family recipe that dates from the 1870s, and is named after the American revolutionary and instigator of the Boston Tea Party. Amber in color, the beer is brewed in the Vienna style. This involves a sedate brewing process that takes forty days. One feature of the Samuel Adams recipe is dry hopping, where extra hops are added as the beer ages.

STRENGTH	4.7% abv
BEER STYLE	Vienna-style lager
ORIGIN	Boston, Massachusetts
TASTE	hoppy and dry

Mexicans have been drinking alcohol for at least 2,000 years, if not longer. The Aztecs made an alcohol called pulque from the fermented juice of the spiky agave plant. They took their pulque drinking seriously: it was part of religion and had a reputation for increasing virility. The chief god of pulque was Two Rabbit, who was said to have an infinite number of sons.

Pulque is still drunk in Mexico, but because it doesn't travel well it's hard to get hold of it any distance from where it's made. The country's real gifts to the world of drink are tequila and mescal, which are distilled from agave plants.

European-style beer arrived in Mexico with the Spanish conqueror Cortes in the 1500s, and Mexico is said to have the first commercial brewery in the Americas. Beer styles today owe more to the influence of German and Austrian immigration during the 1860s—perhaps in part because, before he was shot, Mexico had an Austrian archduke as emperor. These early beers used malt dried in the sun, and had deep, rich colors.

In the past, the only place to drink in Mexico was in a cantina—a hard-

bitten drinking den, where women weren't allowed, and where tequila, mescal, brandy, and very little beer were the order of the day. Cantinas are still part of Mexican drinking culture, but less macho, younger-style cafés and bars are edging them out. Despite the brewing industry being almost totally controlled by two companies, drinkers have a choice —depending on where they are— of around twenty-five kinds of Mexican beer. These include traditional dark styles such as Modelo Negra, which is widely available on export. These beers are often drunk barely chilled.

DOS EQUIS AMBER

Best consumed ice cold, Dos Equis Amber makes a good accompaniment to spicy food. Some drinkers like to add a slice of lemon or lime for extra flavor. It is a Vienna-style reddish beer, with a slightly malty taste typical of the style. Its ingredients include black malt and caramel.

STRENGTH	4.7% abv
BEER STYLE	Vienna-style lager
ORIGIN	Monterrey, Mexico
TASTE	mild, malty taste

Corona Extra is a classic Mexican light beer, and is one of the country's biggest-selling brands. It was first brewed as a cheap, thin beer for modestly paid Mexican workers. With a short lagering time, its worldwide success and cult status is a much-studied phenomenon. This is the beer that started the lime-in-the-neck fashion.

STRENGTH	4.6% abv
BEER STYLE	lager
ORIGIN	Mexico City, Mexico
TASTE	crisp and light

SOL

First brewed in Mexico in 1899 Sol has genuine Mexican credibility. Now produced by Femsa, Sol is actually owned by Belgium-based global brewer Interbrew. A mild, light beer, ideally drunk with a twist of lime, Femsa also brew Superior, a lager with a slightly stronger flavor.

STRENGTH	4.1% abv
BEER STYLE	lager
ORIGIN	Monterrey, Mexico
TASTE	smooth and light

DRINKING IN CHINA

China has one of the oldest cultures on Earth, but beer has arrived only relatively recently. In the late nineteenth century the Germans occupied the northeastern port city of Tsingtao (pronounced ching-dow), across the Yellow Sea from Japan. They brought with them troops, merchants, and a taste for beer, which they supplied by building China's first brewery. China's national beer is still called Tsingtao.

Before beer there was tea, introduced into China around 1,800 years ago. An intricate, involved ritual and culture has grown up around tea, and, for a long time, tea houses filled the same role in Chinese culture as the pub or bar in the west. Now beer rivals tea as the drink of choice, particularly for men and at meal times. There are now hundreds of breweries, and beer is drunk across China. It is frowned upon for women to drink beer in public.

China's other favorite alcohol is a spirit—the traditional mijiu—or a rice spirit called baijiu which is made from sorghum or millet. Serving spirits to guests is regarded as essential for good hospitality, and they are always used for toasts.

Sun Lik is owned by San Miguel, which was originally a Philippino brewery. It is brewed under licence in several countries, including by Shepherd Neame in the UK. The beer sells well in Hong Kong, but its thin taste is designed for the European market. Its ingredients include rice, which partly explains the beer's light body.

STRENGTH	5% abv
BEER STYLE	lager
ORIGIN	Hong Kong, China
TASTE	light with mild hop flavor

The present Tsingtao brewery opened in 1903. One of China's biggest-selling beers and its biggest beer export,Tsingtao is available in some forty countries. It is known as a "rice" beer because rice is added to mashed malt during the brew. The Tsingtao brewery also produce a number of other beers, including a stout.

STRENGTH	4.8% abv
BEER TYPE	pilsner lager
ORIGIN	Tsingtao, China
TASTE	malt with slight hoppy taste

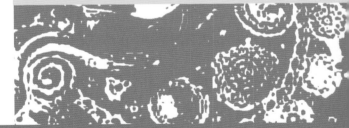

DRINKING IN INDIA

India is the home of distilled alcohol. Barley and rice beer were being distilled by 800 BC—1,800 years before Western Europe discovered the same trick. Today in India there are still many kinds of local home-brewed wines and spirits, such as ragi, made from sweet barley, and toddy, made from palm sap. Everything from jackfruit and mangoes to coconuts and dates is used to make traditional home-brewed alcohol. In the cooler Himalayas region people make and drink chang, which is a beer brewed from millet, and tumba, where fermented millet is mixed with hot water.

Despite India's ancient relationship with alcohol, official and religious attitudes to drinking are not particularly relaxed. Prohibition ruled until relatively recently, and some Indian states, such as Gujarat, still enforce it. Others have partial prohibition, which includes high alcohol taxes and dry days when drinking alcohol is illegal.

Beer in India is a drink for the better off, since it's more expensive than local home brews. In the bigger cities like Mumbai and Delhi there is even something of a pub culture in the British style.

Bangla is produced by the Far Eastern Beer Company, a UK-based concern intended to introduce speciality beers from the Indian sub-continent to the West. Bangla is a relatively sweet and full-bodied lager, aimed at the UK's curry restaurant market. Its name is a contraction of Bangladesh, the original home of many Bengali restaurant owners, though bangla is also the name of a kind of Indian home-brewed alcohol. In the UK Bangla is brewed under contract by a company called Refresh, which is based in Wiltshire.

STRENGTH	5.5% abv
BEER STYLE	pilsner lager
ORIGIN	Trowbridge, Wiltshire, UK
TASTE	clean and crisp

Cobra lager was the idea of Karan Bilimoria, the son of a Gurkha general and a law graduate. First brewed in Bangalore, India, Cobra is double filtered and less gassy than other lagers. Now brewed in the UK by Charles Wells, it is slightly sweeter and less carbonated than other beers of this style.

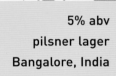

STRENGTH	5% abv
BEER STYLE	pilsner lager
ORIGIN	Bangalore, India
TASTE	slight and crisp

LAL TOOFAN

Lal Toofan is the name of the red dust storm that blows across northern India. This is another beer designed for the Indian restaurant market in the UK. In 2003 it became the first beer to use basmati rice, a rice grown in the fertile soils of the Himalayas, in the brewing process. The nutty flavor of the rice complements the spices found in Indian food.

STRENGTH	5% abv
BEER STYLE	pilsner lager
ORIGIN	Trowbridge, Wiltshire, UK
TASTE	light and crisp

DRINKING IN JAPAN

When thinking of the drinking culture in Japan, sake and whisky immediately spring to mind but, in fact, beer is the really big business. Although there are a few micro breweries in the country sales are dominated by the big breweries and their international-style beer.

It is acceptable for both men and women to drink beer although women are more likely to drink wine. For the young, events worth commemorating are normally celebrated with "ikkinomi"— downing in one. Drinking is normally done from glasses and the important thing to remember is that Japanese etiquette demands that you do not pour your own beer. Rather, you should wait for a friend to pour for you.

In Japan, bars are not required to have a licence and many are open round the clock. If, by some mischance, you can't find a bar that's open there's sure to be a liquor store available round the corner, where the alcohol will undoubtedly be cheaper.

ASAHI DRY

The Asahi (pronounced a-sa-hee) brewery—was the first to introduce bottled beer into Japan, at the beginning of the twentieth century, and then the first to bring in cans, in the 1950s. Asahi Dry was introduced in 1987, and today is one of Japan's top-selling beers. It is a pale international-style lager.

STRENGTH	5% abv
BEER STYLE	lager
ORIGIN	Tokyo, Japan
TASTE	slight, clean flavor

Kirin is named after the half-horse, half-dragon from Chinese mythology that appears on this beer's label. The brewery was founded in the 1870s by an American, and is now one of the largest in the world. Kirin beer is aged for up to two months, and is the brewery's top-selling brand. Kirin also produce a smoke-flavored black beer.

STRENGTH	5% abv
BEER STYLE	pilsner lager
ORIGIN	Tokyo, Japan
TASTE	malt with slight hops

Latin Americans have been making alcohol for more than 2,000 years, and they had beer long before the Spanish conquest. One brew consisted of maize, chewed up and spat into a brewing pot, where it was fermented with water. Tribes in what is now Brazil brewed dark beers from grain and roots.

Some ancient alcohols are still brewed and drunk. In Argentina, chicha, made from fermented monkey puzzle nuts, is popular but hard to get hold of since it's made to be drunk by those who make it. Peru is known for pisco, a fiery white grape brandy. In Brazil, rum made from sugar cane is drunk everywhere, often neat but sometimes as a caipirinha, where it's mixed with crushed ice and lime juice.

European-style brewing arrived in Latin America with the Spanish conquistadors, and then, with nineteenth-century German immigrants, came lager. Today, most Latin American beers are lagers and the most widely drunk beers of all are American-style pale lagers similar to Heineken and Budweiser. However, some individual tastes are still available. In Peru black malt beer is popular,

and in Argentina there's a dark beer called Xingu which is still brewed to an ancient Indian recipe from the Amazon.

Most alcohol drinking takes place in cafés and bars. In Brazil, asking for chopp gets you a draught beer.

Bottled beer often comes in large bottles, 1 pint (600 ml) in Brazil, and in Argentina a 'three quarters' is served. This is meant for sharing, probably a good idea since being publicly drunk in Argentina is regarded as socially unacceptable.

Marketed as the favorite beer of Argentina, Quilmes is a pale golden drink, with a mild international-style flavor in the style of pale lagers such as Budweiser and Heineken. Quilmes is exported widely and has a large slice of the South American beer market.

STRENGTH	5% abv
BEER STYLE	lager
ORIGIN	Buenos Aires, Argentina
TASTE	light with faint trace of malt

BRAHMA CHOPP

The Brazilian Brahma Chopp was first brewed in 1888. Today, it is an ordinary international-style pale lager brewed by AmBev (an Interbrew company), which also makes the lagers Antarctica and Skol.

STRENGTH	5% abv
BEER STYLE	lager
ORIGIN	Rio Grande do Sul, Brazil
TASTE	light with faint bitterness

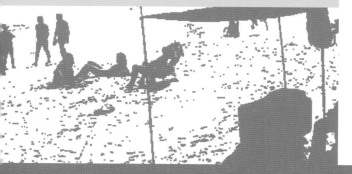

DRINKING IN AFRICA

Africans were the world's first brewers—we know that the ancient Egyptians were fermenting at least four different beers from barley and bread. Western visitors to Africa reported that beer was a vital symbol of prosperity and generosity, and anyone of any importance made sure they had plenty of it around.

Home-brewed beer—brewed to hundreds of different local recipes and tastes—is still central to many African cultures. In fact, there is more home brew than commercial, European-style beer drunk in Africa. In Tanzania, for instance, almost all the alcohol is home brew, with much of it a cloudy, opaque beer made with cassava or maize. In Kenya the national brew is pombe, or bush brew. The recipe varies across the country, and can include millet or banana, along with sugar, roots and herbs for flavor.

In much of Africa home-brewed beer is made and sold by women, and is viewed more as food than drink. In poor communities the kinds of cloudy brews favored provide energy, and B and C vitamins otherwise absent from the diet.

Commercial beer in Africa is mostly bottled pilsner-style beer, some of the best being Tusker Premium from Kenya and Nile Special from neighboring Uganda. In this part of east Africa men on a drinking spree will often fill their table with presents of beer for each other. They will then drink as much as they want, before taking the rest back to the bar to keep for another time.

First brewed in 1896, Castle Lager is now made by the brewing giant South African Breweries—the same people who bring us Carling Black Label. Billed as the friendship brew, Castle Lager is an international-style lager. It was first exported from South Africa in the 1950s, when a few cases reached Mauritius. Castle Lager is now the world's eleventh biggest beer brand, and is sold in over forty countries.

STRENGTH	5% abv
BEER STYLE	lager
ORIGIN	Sandton, South Africa
TASTE	light malt flavor

WINDHOEK LAGER

Namibia Breweries, which was started by German emigrants to the country, still brews Windhoek Lager to the strict standards of the sixteenth-century German purity laws. It has a light, straw color and a grassy aroma.

STRENGTH	4% abv
BEER STYLE	lager
ORIGIN	Windhoek, Namibia
TASTE	good hoppy bitterness with malt

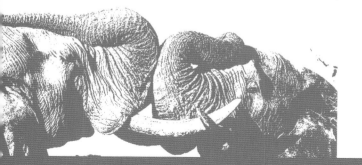

Casablanca is brewed by Morocco's only brewery —itself a subsidiary of Heineken. As a mainly Muslim country without a large market for beer this is brewed mainly for export. It is a mild international-style lager.

STRENGTH	5% abv
BEER STYLE	lager
ORIGIN	Casablanca, Morocco
TASTE	light hop and malt flavor

CONCLUSION

A wine drinker, the Roman emperor Julian was disgusted by north European beer, particularly the stuff from Britain. He was once moved to write a poem on beer which included the line "you smell of goat."

Maybe Julian had just had a bad glass. No matter, beer has endured longer than his poetry, and indeed, the Roman empire. The beautiful drink, smelling of goat or not, lives on. It could easily take a lifetime to find its thousands of different styles and varieties. Of course, that's partly why tasting beer can be such a rewarding hobby.

Acknowledgments

Main Photography by Top That!
Pages 8 and 11: Image Source.
Page 20: Topham Picture Point.
Page 29: Alamy Images.
Pages 35 and 53: Digital Stock.
Page 61: Topham Picture Point.
Page 69: Alamy Images.
Page 87: Stockbyte.
Page 115: Barnabes Bosshart/Corbis.
Page 121: Topham Picture Point.